THE ART
OF GOVERNING

The Art of Governing

JUDD GREGG

★

Flat Rock Books

Flat Rock Books

Distributed by UPNE Book Partners

One Court Street

Lebanon, New Hampshire 03766

ISBN: 978-0-9975801-0-5

© 2016 Judd Gregg

All rights reserved

Manufactured in the

United States of America

*In a democracy,
the art of governing
begins with winning elections.
If you do not win the election,
you do not get to govern.*

THE ESSENTIALS

Know your purpose in wanting to govern.

Set out your purpose. Keep it clear, definable, and understandable.

Build your political persona around your purpose; add integrity, openness, and humor. You will win or at least be comfortable losing.

Have a set of goals, views, and beliefs as the essence of your purpose. Use no more than three or four core themes that everything else feeds off of, such as fiscal restraint, individual liberty, a market economy, and a rational environmental commitment. These will create your identity.

If you have positively set forth your political identity and your purpose, this will guide your actions. People will believe you are doing what you feel is best for them and the country. Thus, even if they disagree, you will have credibility.

Optimism and opportunity are the tone words, build off them.

Say what you think; it will be genuine and easy to defend as honest even if it turns out to be misdirected or wrong. Do not underestimate the power of forthrightness with people.

Be principled but not belligerent or intolerant.

Define your ideological purpose and goals in terms of personal benefit to people.

Do not think that ego and its promotion are substitutes for accomplishment.

The issues of conflict today were identified for the most part by Socrates over two thousand years ago because they are basic human needs and desires. The drivers of governance do not change; they are wealth, power, religion, freedom from want, and liberty. Do not ignore this reality or think you can change it significantly. Work with it.

THE ESSENTIALS OF GOVERNING

Always remember—and remind yourself when confronting issues—that you are not there to further your interests or those of your friends.

There are people who speak to those who make up the ends of the political spectrum. They tend to be shouters. They raise money and they get attention, but they do not govern because they cannot win a majority (and do not wish to govern or win a majority).

There is no such thing as a natural conservative majority or a natural liberal majority. The majority of the American people do not subscribe to the slogans of the left or the right; they subscribe to initiatives and ideas that they see as positively affecting their lives or the community as a whole.

Four types of people seek to govern:

- those who want power
- those who want change
- those who want to do good as they define it
- those who want a job

or those who want some combination of the above.

ESSENTIALS OF GOVERNING: POWER

When power is the essential reason why people seek to govern, governing becomes erratic.

The desire for power through governing is, at its most basic, the desire to be an identifiable individual within a large society.

Power needs to be used as tool of your purpose, not as an end in itself.

In our democracy, power comes from developing and holding majority support.

Much of politics is the march of self-interest of the governing: fame, power, ego, financial gain; this is human nature but it must be tempered by good purpose.

ESSENTIALS OF GOVERNING: EXEMPLIFIED BY THE PRESIDENCY

The Presidency is the most advanced example of governance in our system. It is useful to note these points.

- Great presidents set clear themes that resonate long after they leave office. (Examples: Theodore Roosevelt, Franklin Roosevelt, Ronald Reagan.)
- Great presidents deliver effective leadership in the face of significant potential threats which, by their actions, are muted or aborted. (Examples: Harry Truman, Dwight Eisenhower.)
- Weak presidents leave no wake, no theme or purpose. (Examples: Jimmy Carter, Richard Nixon.)

- Strong presidential leaders have personalities that define and inspire national purpose in a way that makes people identify with national goals.
- Effective presidents lead by knowing and epitomizing the nation's culture and by applying that trait to address issues, often unanticipated by others, in a manner that causes the nation to be a better and safer place.

BASIC RULES OF ENGAGEMENT: THE HIGH GROUND

The political high ground is where you win elections and where you are able to govern effectively.

Seek the political high ground. It consists of ideas and initiatives that people see as:

- producing results
- defending the country
- creating tangible economic benefits like jobs and prosperity
- benefiting the society generally.

For conservatives, seeking the political high ground means convincing people that policies that generate individual initiative also create prosperity, jobs, growth, and liberty.

For liberals, seeking the political high ground means using the government to expand benefits that are seen as generating equality, fairness, and a better life.

During campaigns, as much as possible do negative ads with humor. These are much more effective and memorable— and can maintain the high ground.

When your purpose is both logical and political, talk about the logical and leave others to complain about the political.

BASIC RULES OF ENGAGEMENT: THE REALITY

The left grows its majority by promising benefits to groups who then become part of their coalition. It is insidious but effective. It is why all government moves left.

One of the challenges for conservatives is to show people that benefits are not greater when the government distributes them, but when the individual and a free market energize them.

People are naturally suspicious of the government and government programs in general. But people like their representatives and programs that benefit them directly. To govern well, you need to understand and work with this contradiction.

The distance between thought and action, or a statement and its execution, is a long way.

See things the way they are, not the way you wish they were, then try and change them. But do not be naïve; reality is something you cannot wish away.

Know and remember history; it tends to return in some form. This is an old axiom and true. Very few matters are matters of first impression; learn from others' experiences with similar issues to those you confront.

Too much of the government's work is done as a result of anecdotal needs and stories, or in response to the political fervor of the day, or to retain the position of those in power by creating dependency or giving largess. This usually does not lead to a better-governed society.

Do not personalize the fact that your opponent is flawed; if it is true, others will do it for you.

Public opinion is the fuel of success and the engine of action; keep it on your side.

A loss of public confidence is often the child of a lack of openness.

The U.S. Constitution is not a piece of paper or a theory; it is the bloodstream of everyday governance. Read the Constitution, know it, refer to it, but do not overplay it; tie it to real issues that affect people.

BASIC RULES OF ENGAGEMENT: CONSPIRACIES

Conspiracy theories and theorists always threaten good governance.

A large percentage of people will believe a conspiracy theory if it has some slight grain of accuracy.

Conspiracy theories explain a lot that people do not understand or do not like.

Conspiracy theories often arise because someone in the government does not trust the public with the right to know.

Confront conspiracy theories and their promulgators with openness, logic, facts, and truth. This will allow you to mute the loudest voices who are weaving the conspiracy by undermining them with many of their potential listeners and followers.

Embarrass the demigod with appeals to decency; hold the demigod accountable for his or her claims and the results of his or her actions; do not let them move on from the failures caused by their excesses.

BASIC RULES OF ENGAGEMENT: WHISPERERS AND OTHERS

The most intolerant people you will have to deal with are academics and true believers of both the right and the left; ignore them as best you can.

Watch out for the whisperers; they will tell you that you are doing great, that you are special, that "you should be President." But they just want your attention and consideration for their agenda; do not take their praise too seriously.

COMMUNICATION

Repeat the message.

Do not presume that people know or appreciate good deeds that benefit them; explain those deeds, take credit for them, and then explain them again.

Smile a lot; it is a good message and it is optimistic.

Do not hire the best reporter who covers you as your press person; he or she is much too valuable for that.

Remember that the press are people too; they have families, histories, interests, and favorite sports teams. Learn about them and be agreeable and interested.

When your activities have been commented on, challenged, or attacked in an opinion piece (or an article that expresses opinions), never pass up an opportunity to respond. Newspapers and other legitimate outlets have to run your response as a matter of editorial conscience. This provides you with both free press and visibility.

If you go on MSNBC as a conservative, or FOX as a liberal, be friendly; they hate that.

Today's reporting press is an editorial press, for the most part; it usually wants to use its copy to drive an agenda. Recognize this, live with it, use it if possible, and do not let it upset you; do not swim upstream against it.

The press is often receptive to you doing their job for them by presenting facts and ideas which they can work from. Use this opportunity to create a dialogue and to control, at least in part, the flow of information; to be successful, this information needs to be accurate and not argumentative.

COMMUNICATION: INTERVIEWS

Interviews are where the rubber hits the road in delivering a political message and stating your purposes and themes; work at using them to your advantage.

Do not be drawn off your message.

- Practice your quotable lines so they flow as if original, spontaneous thoughts; in other words, practice being spontaneous.
- Use the quotable phrases that make your points; do not let the interviewer push you into statements that will create the theme of his or her story unless that theme corresponds with yours.
- If an unanticipated interview covers issues about which you have only a first impression, use cautious language.

- Do not exaggerate or expand your language in order to get attention; this usually ends up in quotes that get you in trouble.

In many interviews, you will be just one of numerous people quoted. Because only one or two of your thoughts will make the story, be sure that the quotes you most want to see printed have the more interesting phrasing; keep the rest of the interview bland. If you get off message, it will inevitably be those words that get used.

Stay focused, use zippy language, help the reporter make his or her story interesting.

COMMUNICATION:
A MALICIOUS PRESS

A malicious press person who has an agenda, a cause, and a time slot (or a pen and column) is the most dangerous political person you will have to deal with.

Do not presume that what you know as obviously untrue and misleading is known to anyone else.

Do not let wrong or inaccurate statements go unanswered. They will be repeated, if not immediately, at a later time.

Do not presume you will be given the benefit of the doubt.

Respond to attacks with facts, and third-party testimonials that confirm the facts and your positions.

Point out the inconsistencies and the agenda of the press person's piece to undermine its credibility.

Use tempered outrage and/or humor.

Make your case aggressively. Do not keep the debate going with marginal rebuttals; move on and let it play out.

COMMUNICATION: SOCIAL MEDIA IS THE MESSAGE

Social media is much cheaper and more readily available than all forms of traditional media. If produced by you, it is essentially free press that you can control.

Social media is, however, where the haters hang out.

Social media is where conspiracy theorists breed and are loudest.

In using social media, it is important to manage both the haters and the conspiracy theorists.

Use social media aggressively but read it sparingly, otherwise it will consume your efforts and cause you to lose focus.

In managing social media, hire people who know how to use it, can anticipate its direction and evolution as a political tool, and understand the various audiences and how to speak to them; they will need to translate your purposes, positions, ideas, and goals into the language and presentations that resonate with different users and in different formats.

COMMUNICATION: SPEAKING

If you cannot deliver an effective and engaging speech, then you probably are not going to get the chance to govern and will certainly have trouble developing coalitions of support.

- Know what you want to say; try not to read it.
- Speak using phrases that define your message.
- Adjust your tone depending on your audience, but do not adjust your message.
- Use memorable one-liners and phrases that express your ideas or themes.
- Use facts that give your message substance (and remember that facts are flexible).

- Use stories and anecdotes that are audience-specific; they will draw the interest of the audience and cause it to identify with you.

Make complex issues understandable; practice different approaches to restating complex issues.

Do not green-eyeshade your language. Too many facts and figures will bore an audience; use the strong ones and leave the rest in the shredder.

Practice until you can deliver your key lines, thoughts, and ideas in a comfortable, friendly, and unforced manner.

The goal is to have the audience like you and trust you and your ideas—or at least to respect your commitment to them.

COMMUNICATION: DEBATING

Debating is an art form.

Debates can occasionally win elections but more often lose them.

Debating well can influence the outcome of a vote in a legislature.

Practice your key lines over and over, then throw away the written language and say them naturally.

Save your best comebacks and attack lines for the final rebuttal—that way your opponent does not get to respond immediately.

Never confront your opponent on an issue that you know he or she is ready for and has a good answer to.

Know the facts; know the issues better than your opponent.

Anticipate and practice responses to the unexpected.

Presume that there are no rules your opponent will feel compelled to follow; determine how to respond when such rules are violated.

Treat your opponent with respect, but knock his or her head off with facts or one-liners that you have practiced and can deliver with perfect timing.

If the debate is before an audience, remember that it is body language, body language, body language that often leaves the most lasting positive or negative impression.

There are certain issues that are non-debatable, in the sense that neither side will change position no matter how well the other side presents its case. These issues include abortion and gun control. Simply state your position; do not wear it on your sleeve. Move on to other topics that the political process can actually deal with.

LEGISLATING

In a legislature, you cannot be effective if you do not pass proposals that meet your goals, and you cannot pass proposals if your coalition does not vote together.

In a legislature, it does not take a village—it takes a working majority.

Majority-building in a legislature is personal; know what the people whose support you need really want.

Compromise is considered weakness by those who shout from the corners and claim purity of purpose; in a democracy, built on checks and balances, it is the essence of how things are accomplished.

It is not necessary to forgo one's core values and purposes to reach agreements with those who may hold different values and purposes. It is only necessary to deal with people who understand the need to compromise. This involves arriving at a result that is acceptable to both sides.

Share the microphone. Use the fingerprint approach; the more people who are involved in an idea or a piece of legislation—and who want credit for it—the more likely it is to pass.

Moving forward often requires taking minority positions then building a majority around them through showing how they benefit people in a personal way.

Leading in a legislature means getting people to buy into your purpose; otherwise you are a general without any soldiers.

Count your votes but do not count on your votes (have some in reserve).

In legislating, today's opponent might be tomorrow's ally; make enemies sparingly and choose them purposefully.

If you win a contentious vote, go to your opponent, express admiration for his or her effort, and say you hope to be on the same side on the next issue because he or she is good at what they do. There is no downside to courtesy and respect towards your opponent . . . usually.

Co-opt good ideas. You do not need to be the first to a position or to promote a policy; you need to be the one identified with the position or policy.

Know the rules and procedures better than your opponent and anticipate their uses. See the plays over the horizon—not the next one, but the next ten.

THE UGLIES: FUND-RAISING

Fund-raising is the bane of a candidate or officeholder's day.

Do not raise funds from people who openly want your vote on a certain action; it is not worth it.

Do not make commitments; if people will not contribute without a commitment of some sort, then you cannot afford their support.

Your public positions should be your only commitments.

Fund-raising is fraught with danger and personal peril. Get good people who you trust not to get you in trouble to oversee your fundraising; insist on zero tolerance for bad behavior.

The irony of raising money is that the funds raised do not stay with the candidate but are spent mostly on the media. Thus the people who most often attack candidates and officeholders for raising funds (the members of the media) are the real beneficiaries of that fund-raising—a mystery of politics.

THE UGLIES:
INTEREST GROUPS

Interest groups that have large constituencies who vote—such as veterans, seniors, or realtors—can be formidable opponents and even more formidable allies.

Interest groups deliver people who advocate aggressively. They supply the troops for fighting both for and against issues and actions; use them the way a general would use infantry.

Often it is an interest group's computers that send out the mailings which their members then send on to their representatives, so it becomes their computers talking to your computers. Get past this. Meet with their membership, especially the rank and file, and make your case one-on-one as often as possible.

An interest group's national leadership is often driven primarily by the need to stress issues that energize fund-raising (and gives them a job). There is not a great deal of idealism in this exercise; actions and positions are often driven by the self-interest of the national staff.

Interest groups are not monolithic; the people who lead the groups in your state are usually reasonable and willing to work with you even if the national leadership disagrees with you. Cultivate the local leadership, communicate regularly with them, and explain your positions and actions. If your position is at odds with that of the national leadership, then go directly to the people affected in your state.

LOBBYISTS

Lobbyists are not confidants; they are part of the fabric of governing. They give support and want access; they have and convey knowledge; they hope and expect it will be used to promote their purposes.

Use, do not be used by, lobbyists.

Access is the currency of lobbyists.

Lobbyists are paid to get information from you and to convince you that you need the information they have and should support the positions they espouse.

Lobbyists are useful; they raise money and give information on complex issues.

Lobbyists are whisperers and repeaters of rumors. They get paid to do this; listen to them skeptically.

It is a two-way street: elected officials and candidates should take advantage of lobbyists' knowledge and their fund-raising, but they should do this with their eyes open, without expecting that this involves trust or that confidences can be shared without risk.

Lobbyists are not friends; consultants are not friends. They are paid to act like friends and friends are not paid.

Lobbyists generally have a very low opinion of members of Congress and state legislatures and believe that they can be manipulated. If members knew how they were viewed by most lobbyists, then they would never talk to them—but they need their fund-raising, and sometimes their knowledge, so the dance goes on.

Lobbyists are not bad people; they are simply hired folks whose allegiance is transitory. They are the mercenaries of the political class. It is important to realize this, as they are a ubiquitous part of the body politic and, if dealt with intelligently, can be very helpful.

LEADERSHIP

Governing is accomplished by many but the many require one, defining leader who gives them direction, purpose, and cohesion.

Leadership does not stop with the leader. It must go down the line if it is to have an impact at the point where action occurs.

Coalitions are the engines of legislation (and of winning elections), but they require strong leadership to give them cohesion and direction.

Actions on policies that involve large programs and affect many people—such as Social Security, Medicare, or tax reform—will only be accepted if people see them as fair. In our form of government, only bipartisan actions on these large issues are seen as fair.

Pick good staff; give them running room so they are motivated to produce good ideas and results, but give them direction as to your purpose so they do not go off on tangents or waste your time.

Do not turn big issues over to other people; you will end up defending something with your name on it that may not be what you really wanted. Everyone has agendas—even your closest staff.

Know your resources, which are primarily people, and use them effectively.

- Do not undermine the morale of the key delivers of services.
- Do not pander.
- Give clear directions with clear expectations and act when they are not met.

If you are a chief executive, such as a governor, for every action there is a reaction and things get done.

If you are in a legislature, for every action there is a rerun of the action. It is like working with Jell-O. It takes patience and perseverance to move an issue forward and get action.

Good government gets things done—practical things that benefit people at a cost that can be justified because of the positive nature of the outcome.

BUREAUCRACIES

Bureaucracies govern; governing bureaucracies is the key to getting things done.

For broad social policies to work, they must include a means for the policy drivers (the elected governing class) to control, direct, get support from, and get positive action from those who execute the policies (the bureaucracy).

The challenge of managing the bureaucracy is at the center of having government actively accomplish good things and be a constructive force in building a better society.

A complacent bureaucracy can fritter all your good purposes and intentions away.

Bureaucracies tend to play rope-a-dope with elected officials, as bureaucrats know they will most likely be there long after the elected official moves on.

In bureaucracies, there is no reward for productivity or good results, only for showing up and not messing up. (This does not apply to those working in national security areas.)

Trying to change the culture of a bureaucracy goes against human nature, thus it is a challenge and is not accomplished easily.

Legislative purpose and intent can be easily corrupted by bureaucratic execution, which can be excessive, misapplied, purposefully indifferent, or purposefully misinterpreted.

Those who serve in areas such as labor or environmental protection come to work with their own purposes and causes and often ignore the elected executive or legislative intent and purpose.

It is difficult for conservatives to have a responsive bureaucracy because the nature of conservative goals is to rein in or limit government and thus the bureaucracy. This challenges the power of the bureaucrat and thus his or her status and causes a natural resistance to conservative governance.

To manage bureaucracies, a message of accountability must come from the elected leadership.

Public visibility is one of the best ways to get accountability. Give the public information regarding the quality and effectiveness of services and government activities.

The message from the top must be that the bureaucracy must act ethically.

Replace those who are not doing their jobs well, in a public way if necessary, in order to deliver the message that a better job of governing is expected.

Publicly and regularly reward and acknowledge those who give exceptional service.

RULES GOVERNING GOVERNING

Intellectual or academic solutions to complex problems often lead to unintended consequences that defy and undermine those solutions.

Watch out for smart people who think they are smart, as they tend to govern and write laws in a way that tells other people how to live their lives. It usually turns out that they are wrong and their laws and actions are resented.

The arrogance of those who think of themselves as the governing elite is almost limitless; in the name of good causes and political correctness, they produce a constant flow of disastrous policies.

Avoid belligerent people; if you cannot avoid them, then expose them as foolish, out of step, or a detriment to the majority of people they are addressing.

Themes and purpose set tone, but procedure and details determine outcomes; focus on both.

Do not pick political fights unless you know the consequences and potential results and can control both.

If you have an issue or a problem you wish to obfuscate, appoint a commission to consider it. Act like its findings are important; ignore what you do not like and use what you do like.

CRISIS

Your goals and purposes can be sidetracked and supplanted by crisis; the management of crises will greatly impact your success in governing.

It is the things that seem little—often unnoticed or only casually noticed on first impression—that can end up causing the most political harm. These often involve someone's personal tragedy; but just because it does not seem like a large event does not mean it is not going to become important. Pause and consider their needs, and the event's implications, before moving on.

When you do realize you have a problem, move quickly to diffuse it, even if it is inconvenient or politically difficult.

In a major, obvious crisis:

- take immediate, visible control
- explain the situation to the public
- explain the options for action to the public
- ACT.

THE WAY IT ENDS

If you follow your purposes you will govern effectively but, in the end, what matters the most is that you come through your time of governing with your dignity, integrity, and family.

ABOUT THE AUTHOR

JUDD GREGG served as a U.S. representative for the state of New Hampshire from 1981 to 1989, as governor from 1989 to 1993, and as a United States senator from 1993 to 2011. He and his wife, Kathleen MacLellan, live in Rye Beach, New Hampshire. They have three children and four grandchildren.